From here to there

How do you get from here
to there? Do you go by bus,
ship or a hot-air balloon?

There are lots of different forms of transport.

My dad is a farmer and
we travel by oxcart. The
cart is pulled by oxen.

My mum and I are jetting off on a long flight. It is the quickest form of travel.

If you are in Japan, you might like to go on a high-speed train.

But if you are not in a rush, then paddling on a river or lagoon is fun.

If you have a lot of canals and not a lot of streets, then floating on a boat is best.

My pals and I travel into town like this. We can coast downhill and pick up speed.

In a hot desert, I go
by camel. I sit up high
and can see far off.

This is my transport – hoof power! It is so much fun to gallop by the trees.

My arms have a lot of power! I can do all sorts of sports in my chair too.

In the summer, my dad and I like going to the park on our scooters.

In Finland, dogs help me zoom along. Sledding is cool!

I go by car. My dog has a need for speed! She loves the wind.

How do you go?

Words to blend

different	transport	travel
quickest	paddling	best
Finland	sledding	farmer
balloon	lagoon	power
desert	jetting	sports
chair	park	zoom
wind	town	cart

Before reading

Synopsis: There are so many ways to travel. Some of them are fast and some are slow. Which ones have you experienced?

Review graphemes/phonemes: igh ee ai oa oo er or

Book discussion: Look at the cover and read the title together. Ask: *What do you think this book will be about? Is it fiction or non-fiction? How do you know?* Elicit that non-fiction books like this one often have photos rather than drawn artwork.

Link to prior learning: Display a word with adjacent consonants from the story, e.g. *streets*. Ask children to put a dot under each single-letter grapheme (*s, t, r, t, s*) and a line under the digraph (*ee*). Model, if necessary, how to sound out and blend the adjacent consonants together to read the word. Repeat with another word from the story, e.g. *floating*, and encourage children to sound out and blend the word independently.

Vocabulary check: lagoon – a saltwater lake

Decoding practice: Write these words on cards: *flight, train, coast, trees, sports*. Hold up one card at a time for children to read. Encourage fluent reading on sight, without overt sounding out and blending, as far as possible.

Tricky word practice: Display the word *our* and ask children to circle the tricky part of the word (*ou*, which makes the /ow/ sound). Practise writing and reading this word.

After reading

Apply learning: Ask: *Which of the methods of transport in the book have you tried before? Which would you most like to try, and why?*

Comprehension

- Where might you find high-speed trains?

- In which country do they enjoy sledding?

- Can you name two methods of transport in the book that involve animals?

Fluency

- Pick a page that most of the group read quite easily. Ask them to reread it with pace and expression. Model how to do this if necessary.

- Children could choose a favourite page to read aloud. Can they make their reading sound natural and fluent?

- Practise reading the words on page 17.

Tricky words review

our	loves	here
there	do	you
go	by	pull
like	into	so
all	me	she